DMS ColourScene 1979 – 1984

N. J. Eadon-Clarke

DTS Publishing

ABOVE: Where it all began. The sight that greeted me at the Grays premises of Ensignbus on the first weekend that they acquired DMSs from London Transport. Left to Right: DMSs 1251/6/8, 1261/60/59/55/63/62. Most of these vehicles had been in LT service the previous week.
13 May 1979

LEFT: These four DMSs 1261/60/59/55 seen at Grays would all see further service with WMPTE.
13 May 1979

BELOW: DMS 1265 seen in the Grays yard next to former East Kent KFN220. This DMS would be one of the initial four licenced for further use by City of Oxford Motor Services Ltd in August 1979.
13 May 1979

ABOVE: DMS 1250 did not survive and was scrapped in Barnsley within a couple of months of this view at the Grays yard of Ensignbus. Also seen is ex LCBS SM116 and ex East Kent OFN732F.
13 May 1979

RIGHT: DMS 1266 withdrawn in the rear yard of Bromley garage awaiting collection. This bus would not survive much longer, being scrapped in Barnsley a few months later.
19 May 1979

BELOW: DMS 1268 leaves LT premises for the last time. It is being driven under trade plates by an Ensignbus driver. This bus would see further service with WMPTE.
21 May 1979

LEFT: DMS 1266 is the second of four DMSs to be collected by Ensignbus from Bromley garage on this date.
21 May 1979

BELOW: DMS 1267 leaves Bromley garage for the last time. It is being driven under trade plates by an Ensignbus driver. This bus would be re-licensed within 3 months with its new owner, City of Oxford Motor Services Ltd.
21 May 1979

BOTTOM: The final DMS to be collected by Ensignbus from Bromley garage on this day was DMS 1264. The blue smoke shows that the engine is still cold as it roars away for a new life with WMPTE.
21 May 1979

TOP: Two DMSs in the Grays yard of Ensignbus that would both see further service. DMS 1267 would be in service in Oxford within two months. DMS 1256 would retain LT livery and enter service on the Round London Sightseeing Tour with dealer E Brackell before passing to Hewitts Farm in Orpington.

3 June 1979

ABOVE: DMS 1276 a former Bromley bus is seen crossing Waterloo bridge during a road run connected with the 1979 London Bus Rally. The bus carries the livery of its new owner WMPTE.

22 July 1979

LEFT: DMS 1257 displays its new livery for WMPTE at the 1979 London Bus Rally in Brockwell Park Lambeth, note the very limited destination blind display.

22 July 1979

LEFT: DMS 1276 arrives at Brockwell Park after completing its road run through London as part of the 1979 London Bus Rally. This vehicle looks exceptionally smart and tidy in its new WMPTE livery. **22 July 1979**

BELOW: Inside DMS 1276 showing the layout after removal of the centre door. The early conversions had an inwards facing seat where the doors had been and the space formerly occupied by the AFC machine is now a luggage pen. **22 July 1979**

LEFT: Former DMS 1256 now with E Brackell caused quite a surprise when it entered service on the Round London Sightseeing Tour under contract to LT. It is seen in Whitehall passing a Mk1 Ford Escort. **22 July 1979**

LEFT: DMS 1260 outside the yard of Ensignbus at Grays awaiting final checks before making its way to Birmingham.
12 August 1979

BELOW: Three more DMSs await their fate in the Grays yard of Ensignbus. DMSs 1291 & 1297 would both be scrapped, but 1294 far left in this view would make the journey to Birmingham to become WMPTE 5525.
12 August 1979

LEFT: On Page 2 we saw DMS 1265 in the yard of Ensignbus at Grays. By August it was in service with City of Oxford Motor Services and is seen here in Oxford city centre looking extremely smart in NBC red.
22 August 1979

LEFT: Alongside CMB DMS 438 at Sandpits we see DMS 1414 which was being used by Ensignbus as a demonstrator to potential buyers. After various owners in the UK DMS 1414 passed to Chicago Motor Coach where it was extensively renovated in early 1995 by Leon Daniels, it is believed to still exist in 2001.
13 April 1980

LEFT: Nearside view of DMS 1414 at Sandpits during the 1980 Cobhan Rally with adverts for Ensignbus.
13 April 1980

RIGHT: Red Rover of Aylesbury acquired two DMSs in 1979 and more later. In this view we see DMS 419 parked in the doorway of their garage in their attractive livery devoid of adverts.
24 April 1980

TOP: The second DMS with Red Rover was DMS 437. Here we see it entering Aylesbury Town centre as Red Rover no. 139. This bus would see service with Red Rover for almost six years before going to Stevensons for spares.
24 April 1980

ABOVE: DMS 437 enters the gloomy Bus Station in Aylesbury showing a rear advert for the associated Keith Garages Ltd and the retention of the panels above the engine compartment.
24 April 1980

LEFT: Lancashire United Transport placed an order with Ensignbus for twenty DMSs. Here we see DMS 597 outside their Grays yard ready to make the journey north to become LUT No. 318, although not numerically the first this bus was one of the first batch to be licensed with LUT.
18 May 1980

LEFT: DMS 597 outside Ensignbus at Grays, ready to head north to become LUT No. 318. The centre door removal can be seen to be similar to that carried out on the West Midlands vehicles.
18 May 1980

RIGHT: On Page 2 we saw DMS 1261 in the yard of Ensignbus. In this view in Navigation Street, Birmingham we see it in service with WMPTE. Note the blind display has been enlarged from that originally planned see photos on page 5.
23 May 1980

LEFT: DMS 1273 stands in Navigation Street, Birmingham, the terminus of route 63, note the 'T' shape destination blind with the route number shown twice.
23 May 1980

RIGHT: DMS 1270 is seen inside the West Midlands PTE garage at Selly Oak alongside a Mk1 metrobus and a Leyland National.
23 May 1980

BELOW: DMS 1272 is also seen inside West Midlands PTE garage at Selly Oak claiming to be 'special'.
23 May 1980

RIGHT: DMS 1310 pauses opposite West Midlands PTE Selly Oak garage in Harbourne Lane. This bus would return to Ensignbus in 1986 and see further service with Lambkin on the isle of Sheppey.
23 May 1980

LEFT: DMS 1279 now WMPTE 5516 outsi Selly Oak garage showing the rear end tre ment and the retention of the panels above t engine compartment.
23 May 1980

BELOW: Numerically the first DMS in t WMPTE fleet, number 5550, DMS 1255 stan outside Selly Oak garage.
23 May 1980

BOTTOM: DMS 1278 now West Midlan PTE No. 5515 stands on the forecourt of Se Oak garage alongside a Metrobus and Leyla National.
23 May 1980

LEFT: DMS 1276 was pictured at the 1979 London Bus Rally (see page 6). Here it is again in traffic in selly Oak High Street on route 2.

23 May 1980

BELOW: DMS 1271 in Market Place, Selly Oak as WMPTE 5510, note the one line destination display.

23 May 1980

LEFT: DMS 1329 now WMPTE 5551 is seen in Victoria Square, Birmingham followed by a standard Birmingham fleetline.

23 May 1980

LEFT: Colmore Row, Birmingham sees DMS 1317 with the original restricted destination display, en route to Quinton, one of three garages that originally received an allocation of DMSs.

23 May 1980

BELOW: Three months after entering service with WMPTE and still gleaming, DMS 1349 is seen in Colmore Row on route 10.

23 May 1980

BOTTOM: DMS 1354 now WMPTE 5565 passes another fleetline in Colmore Row Birmingham. This bus was later to become a playbus in Birmingham before passing to New York Apple Tours where it served as a static ticket office for many years.

23 May 1980

ABOVE: DMS 1358 now WMPTE 5570 is seen in Bull Street, Birmingham. This bus would later return to the South East and be one of the four examples that operated for Harris of Grays.
23 May 1980

LEFT: DMS 1338 now WMPTE 5557 picks up passengers in Corporation Street, Birmingham.
23 May 1980

LEFT: The first of many DMSs to be converted to open top. DMS 1304 is seen at the Derby on Epsom Downs in the ownership of Smiths Luxury Coaches (Reading) Ltd, but in the livery of associated company Windsorian Coaches were it is normally to be found on sightseeing tours in Windsor. This bus still exists with Guide Friday, but is currently in secure storage.
4 June 1980

LEFT: Between December 1979 and July 1980 Derby City Transport received eight DMSs from Ensign. These included four of the original five experimental examples fitted with front two piece glider doors and just one example bodied by MCW. Here DMS 465 with glider front doors rests at the garage, the centre door removal is similar to that carried out to WMPTE example.

22 July 1980

CENTRE LEFT: One of the seven PRV bodied DMSs acquired by Derby City Transport DMS 441 is now Derby 254 which is one of only two with four piece front doors. It stands in the bright sunshine in the garage yard.

22 July 1980.

RIGHT: Chesterfield Borough Council Transport were another early customer for DMSs from Ensign, taking sixteen examples with equal numbers of bodies by PRV and MCW. DMS 1415 was the third vehicle licenced in June 1980. It is seen here one month later with gleaming paintwork opposite the bus station.

22 July 1980

LEFT: DMS 568 was the second bus into service with Chesterfield Borough Council Transport being licenced in June 1980. It stands opposite the bus station showing its smart livery to good effect. Note the new traffic indicators fitted to Chesterfield vehicles.
22 July 1980

BELOW: The scene in the yard of Wombwell Diesels showing various LT and LCBS vehicles being reduced to strips of metal. The unidentified DMS in the centre is thought to be either DMS 1534 or DMS 1416.
22 July 1980

BOTTOM: The remains of a DMS and SMS in the yard of Wombwell Diesels.
22 July 1980

LEFT: On the day of my visit the proprietor of Wombwell Diesels forbade the taking of photographs. Hence this view of DMS 734 taken through the car windscreen.

22 July 1980

RIGHT: DMS 1285, now WMPTE 5519 picks up passengers in Navigation Street Birmingham almost one year after entering service with WMPTE the lower panels are showing signs of damage.

6 August 1980

LEFT: By 1980 sales of PRV bodied DMSs were increasing. Here in the Grays yard of Ensignbus we see DMS 653 being prepared for use at Dover docks by Townsend Thoresen. DMSs 405 & 399 would both make the trip to China Motor Bus in Hong Kong.

25 August 1980

ABOVE: This unique view show the initial three DMSs ordered by Chung Wah Shipbuilding in Hong Kong in the Grays yard of Ensignbus. Left to right they are DMS 663, 626 & 606. The green and white livery carried by 626 which was to become Chung Wah No 1 was not retained in Hong Kong. **25 August 1980**

BELOW: This nearside view of DMS 663 in the grays yard of Ensignbus clearly shows the removal of the centre doors and reduced width front door. In front of it is DMS 1364 one of the final vehicles being prepared for WMPTE. **25 August 1980**

LEFT: The 1980 Showbus rally took place at Thorpe Park, a venue not used again due to the high entrance cost. The opportunity was taken to line up a number of DMSs in their new liveries. Here we see DMS 196 with Stevensons of Uttoxeter next to DMS 653 which would shortly enter service with Townsend Thoreson. Stevensons obtained many of their DMSs as non runners or from scrap yards and rebuilt them in their Spath workshops. DMS 196 was one such vehicle having been obtained from scrapyard of Wombwell Diesels.

7 September 1980

LEFT: 1980 Showbus rally at Thorpe Park. Next to Townsend Thoresen DMS 653 is DMS 1402 with Charlton Services which served Charlton-on-Otmoor for the following nine years.

7 September 1980

BELOW: 1980 Showbus rally at Thorpe Park. DMS 1371 with City of Oxford Motor Services which was later to see service with Southend Transport and Black Horse of Catford next to DMS 1307 converted to a mobile exhibition unit with Ciba Geigy with whom it would serve for an incredible 17 years before being given in return for services rendered to another company for further use.

7 September 1980

RIGHT: DMS 415 at the 1980 Showbus Rally in its first livery with Hedingham & District Omnibuses, it would later receive a revised livery before passing back to Ensignbus for further service in 1988.

7 September 1980

RIGHT: 1980 Showbus rally, DMS 624 appeared in LT livery and was later burnt out for a motion picture, Next to it is the first open top DMS 1304 taking a break from sightseeing work in Windsor.

7 September 1980

BELOW: Line up of various DMSs at the 1980 Showbus rally at Thorpe Park.

7 September 1980

ABOVE LEFT: Ensignbus at Grays. DMS 695 receives a chassis repaint prior to its despatch to Kowloon Motor Bus in Hong Kong. **26 October 1980**

ABOVE: DMS 1526 is seen parked outside the yard of Ensignbus at Grays, being prepared for further service with Western National. This bus would have long life seeing service with WNOC, Midland Red North and Kime's Coaches of Folkingham before returning to London for use on sightseeing with the Big Bus company. **26 October 1980**

LEFT: DMS 626 seen outside the Ensignbus yard in Grays ready for despatch to Chung Wah Shipbuilding in Hong Kong where it would become their fleet number 1. This livery would not however survive, it being repainted before entry into service. **26 October 1980**

LEFT: Many DMSs suffered this fate, ie having useful parts removed to support other vehicles before being sent for scrap. DMS 1581 is seen here outside Ensignbus at Grays with most windows removed prior to scrapping the following month. **28 June 1981**

ABOVE: Several DMSs became driver trainers with LCBS for a couple of years before passing to Midland Red East for further service. DMS 641 is seen on training work in Central London, Southampton Row.

3 July 1981

LEFT: Bedlington & District of Ashington purchased 16 DMSs for use on colliery contracts. A daytrip from Kent to Ashington was required and proved somewhat disappointing when on arrival I found all the vehicles were tightly parked and with the sun directly behind them. In this view we can see DMSs 555 and 1252 with1298 behind.

1 August 1981

LOWER LEFT: DMS 1475 seen outside the workshop of Bedlington & District at Ashington. This was the newest DMS purchased and lasted until 1991, a very credible period given that many of the roads in the area suffered from severe subsidence.

1 August 1981

ABOVE: The front line of DMSs parked at the Ashington yard of Bedlington & District. From left to right are DMSs 422, 1448, 561 and 416. DMS 1448 is named Big Geordie and DMS 561 is named Rock-on-Tommy on their lower front panels.

1 August 1981

LEFT: Close up view of two Bedlington & District DMSs in the rear line at Ashington showing the Daimler badge and name JIM'LL-FIX-IT on DMS 1263 next to DMS 1423. DMS 1263 was pictured in the yard of Ensign on Page 2.

1 August 1981

LOWER LEFT: Big Geordie (DMS 1448) and Rock-on-Tommy (DMS 561) seen in the Ashington yard of Bedlington & District.

1 August 1981

LEFT: DMS 416 in the yard of Bedlington & District at Ashington. This bus later passed to Struan Motors of Perth in Scotland for use as an exhibition vehicle and is still used in that role. It was the only vehicle out of the 16 DMSs owned to see further use, the remainder were all scrapped.

1 August 1981

LEFT: DMSs 555 and 1252 in the Ashington yard of Bedlington & District these vehicles saw ten and eight years service respectively before being withdrawn and scrapped.

1 August 1981

RIGHT: Wiffen's Coaches of Finchingfield Essex purchased DMS 677 in January 1981 and it is seen here parked in their yard next to the village green. Later in the year they purchased a second example.

19 August 1981

ABOVE: Three types of vehicle parked in the yard of Stevensons at Spath, on the left former Northern General Routemaster RCN 699, on the right former Maidstone Corporation Atlantean JKE335E and in the middle DM 1708 now Stevensons No. 31.

29 August 1981

LEFT: DMS 314 was another DMS purchased from the scrapyard of Wombwell Diesels and refurbished for further service by Stevensons. It is seen here in the Spath workshops with a newly painted engine.

29 August 1981

LOWER LEFT: DMS 298 again seen in Uttoxeter bus station as Stevensons No. 48 carrying the stripey livery and a side painted advert for the availability of 73 seated buses for hire.

29 August 1981

ABOVE: I travelled from Uttoxeter to Burton on Trent on board DMS 457, which is seen here awaiting departure from Uttoxeter bus station. **29 August 1981**

BELOW: DMS 241 now Stevensons 47 seen in Uttoxeter bus station in stripey livery with side painted advert for Stevensons express services to Birmingham. **29 August 1981**

ABOVE: City of Oxford Motor Services No. 997, DMS 1352 seen on the Park & Ride service in a congested Cornmarket Street.
12 September 1981

RIGHT: DMS 1274 now City of Oxford Motor services No. 993 seen opposite the Cowley Road garage in NBC red livery.
12 September 1981

RIGHT: DMS 1343 now City of Oxford Motor Services No. 995 seen in Oxford in full Park & Ride livery picking up a full load of weary shoppers.
12 September 1981

LEFT: A very wet day in Wood Street Cardiff sees DMS 1552 of CK Coaches. An early example of a low fare bus company competing with the incumbent large operator. The operation lasted little over one year.

17 October 1981

BELOW: DMS 1584 is seen in Wood Street Cardiff in the rain operating for CK coaches. When the company ceased to trade the following year this bus saw further service with Cottrell's Coaches of Mitcheldean and then Stevensons of Uttoxeter.

17 October 1981

BOTTOM: CK Coaches DMS 1586 seen in the rain in Wood Street Cardiff. This bus would pass through the hands of several operators after CK ceased trading in 1982.

17 October 1981

LEFT: The first of many DMSs purchased by Cityrama for London Sightseeing tours was DM 1765. It is seen here at Victoria station in original condition retaining its roof.
31 October 1981

BELOW: By October 1981 Grimsby-Cleethorpes Joint Transport Committee had five DMSs licensed, but a trip to Grimsby was very disappointing with only one former London vehicle seen. This was DMS 792 seen here in the new caramel and cream livery in Riby Square, Grimsby.
21 November 1981

LEFT: The attractive livery of Lodge's of High Easter is seen on DMS 1601 at the North Weald bus rally in 1982. This bus was later to receive an even more attractive livery.
30 May 1982

RIGHT: Derby day 1982 sees DMS1692 providing hospitality services whilst in the ownership of Jobs Dairies of Hanworth. The bus carries the name Lady Louisa and would be a regular visitor to Epsom Downs on Derby day.
2 June 1982

BELOW: A unique DMS seen at the Southend bus rally. Ensignbus converted DMS 729 into a LHD demonstrator in an effort to stimulate interest from buyers overseas. The bus also has other additional features such as twin headlights and new traffic indicators. No other LHD conversions took place and this bus ended its days with Chicago Motor Coach.
6 June 1982

LEFT: For many years Ensignbus supplied buses to act as rally control vehicles at the entrance to the Southend bus rally. In 1982 the role was performed by DMS 2163 and DMS 2066. Later that year 2163 would pass to Stevensons of Uttoxeter before becoming the first of many DMSs in the fleet of Mayne's of Manchester. 2066 would pass to Maidstone & District the following year.
6 June 1982

ABOVE: By 1982 Ensignbus had moved from Grays to larger premises next to the A13 at Purfleet. DM 1107 and DM 1018 stand in their yard. Both buses were sent for scrap without seeing further use.
17 July 1982

RIGHT: DM 927 being prepared for China Motor Bus of Hong Kong in the Purfleet yard of Ensignbus. This bus would become CMB XF 136.
17 July 1982

RIGHT: A view of the Ensignbus Purfleet workshops taken from the doorway. The open top bus on the left DMs 2150 would be exported to TSW of Hong Kong who would lease it to Citybus. It was the first permanent Open Top bus in Hong Kong and new upper deck guard rails are being fitted here. DMS 1662 would re-enter service with Gastonia Coaches of Cranleigh. (see page 72). It may be of passing interest to learn that while the Author was photographing DMS 2150 at Purfleet, the publisher was awaiting its arrival in Hong Kong where he was them the manager of TSW (Hong Kong) Limited.
17 July 1982

LEFT: Another DMS seen in the Purfleet yard of Ensignbus that would become unique. In an apprentices exercise DM 1758 would have its wheelbase shortened and then be used within the yard for storage and shunting duties.

17 July 1982

CENTRE LEFT: DMSs lined up for attention in the Purfleet workshops of Ensignbus, both identifiable DMs will end up in Hong Kong, DM 961 will become CMB XF 137 and DM 1780 will be Argos No. 12.

17 July 1982

BELOW: The scene outside the Purfleet workshop of Ensignbus with DMS 1667 in the foreground.

17 July 1982

RIGHT: DM 1778 seen inside the Midland Fox East garage at Wigston looking every bit like a new modern bus.
28 August 1982

CENTRE RIGHT: Chesterfield Borough Council Transport held a garage open day in 1982. The inside display of vehicles included DMS 568 and DMS 1412 both carrying 'Not to go out' notices in their front windscreens.
25 September 1982

BELOW: The workshop area of Stonegravels depot of Chesterfield Borough Council Transport during their 1982 open day sees DMS 1432 over the pits. After being retired by Chesterfield this bus would see further service in North Wales with Voel Coaches.
25 September 1982

LEFT: SYPTE 1511 a DMS style fleetline passes Chesterfield Stonegravels depot. This bus would later be exported to Hong Kong for operation alongside other DMSs in the fleet of Argos.
25 September 1982

LEFT: Rear view of DMS 1428 now Chesterfield Borough Council Transport No. 165 in Elder Way Chesterfield.
25 September 1982

BELOW: DM1211 was the newest DMS purchased by Chesterfield Borough Council Transport in whose fleet it was No. 175, it was also the last to be withdrawn in spring 1991. It then saw further service with Camms of Nottingham and Euroline of Nottingham. Here it picks up passengers in Elder Way, Chesterfield.
25 September 1982

ABOVE: DM1211 seen in Knifesmithgate Chesterfield with the world famous Chesterfield spire ahead of it.
25 September 1982

RIGHT: DMS 744 now Chesterfield Borough Council Transport No. 171 picks up passengers in Vicar Lane bus station.
25 September 1982

RIGHT: Chesterfield Borough Council Transport No. 163, DMS 1417 seen in Vicar Lane bus station. This bus would later see use with the Retford & District subsidiary where it would receive a blue and yellow livery.
25 September 1982

LEFT: Chesterfield Borough Council Transport No. 168, DMS 1443 seen in New Beetwell Street Chesterfield, eight years later this bus would pass to Enterprise & Silver Dawn Bus Company in Lincoln for further service.
25 September 1982

LEFT: DMS 1434 now Chesterfield Borough Council Transport No. 169 in Beetwell Street showing the diagonal panel inserted by Chesterfield above the engine compartment. This was a relatively rare modification, most operators simply removing the original inserts.
25 September 1982

BELOW: With Chesterfield's famous spire in the background DMS 759 now Chesterfield Borough Council Transport No. 172 speeds along Lordsmill. After just over eight years service with Chesterfield this bus would spend another eight productive years with Voel coaches in North Wales.
25 September 1982

TOP: DMS 706 now Chesterfield Borough Council Transport No. 173 seen in Lordsmill Chesterfield.
25 September 1982

ABOVE: Also seen in Lordsmill Chesterfield, DMS 738 now Chesterfield Borough Council Transport No. 174.
25 September 1982

RIGHT: Chesterfield Borough Council Transport No. 160, DMS 553 the first DMS to be purchased in 1980 and also numerically the first of the batch. After nine years use in Chesterfield this vehicle would spend another two years with a film support company before being scrapped in autumn 1993.
25 September 1982

RIGHT: DM 1785 would see ten years use in Leicester. It is seen here in Charles Street Leicester in the autumn sunshine in its original condition.
3 October 1982

CENTRE: DMS 2061 was another of the three vehicles purchased by London Cityrama in 1982 which entered service with its roof intact. It stands at the Victoria station start point for their tour of London.
6 November 1982

LEFT: Following the success of the three vehicles purchased in 1982, London Cityrama followed up that purchase with a further four vehicles in 1983. DMS 2127 was one of the 1983 deliveries and is seen at Victoria. This bus still exists in open top form can be seen during the summer months providing visitor transport in the grounds of Whipsnade Zoo.
7 April 1983

ABOVE: DMS 1424 was to have an eventful life operating with many subsequent owners. Here it is in the ownership of Obsolete Fleet and is working on the Round London Sightseeing Tour in Victoria Street. The application of white around the upper deck windows was made to match the livery application to much newer DMSs with London Transport.

7 April 1983

LEFT: Derelict DMS 1693 was the unfortunate victim at the 1983 North Weald bus rally to demonstrate how to recover an overturned bus. Not surprisingly this bus was subsequently sent for scrap.

22 May 1983

LOWER LEFT: Derby day 1983 and the best photo possible of DMS 178 accompanying other vehicles from the hospitality fleet of Bus Fare of Cranleigh.

1 June 1983

ABOVE: Red Rover Omnibus Company acquired DMS 2233 in May 1983. One of its first duties was a trip to the Derby, it stands amongst other double deckers next to the racecourse.

1 June 1983

LEFT: The only photograph of DMS 701 that I was able to obtain was this view taken at the Derby while it was in the ownership of Blue Lake Central Bus & Coach Hire, Chichester.

1 June 1983

LEFT: DMS 571 was another elusive vehicle passing to the Womens Peace Bus Co-operative, Brixton and was reported painted black with coloured circles and sometimes stored in Clapham garage. It is seen before sale from Ensign at the Southend rally.

5 June 1983

ABOVE: DMS 2091 a 1983 delivery to London Cityrama passes St. Paul's Cathedral with converted DMS 2148 in the background.

6 August 1983

LEFT: Another 1983 purchase by London Cityrama was DMS 2104 seen passing St. Paul's cathedral. After serving in London this bus was exported to New York.

6 August 1983

BELOW: Another bus to end its days in New York was DM 1720, here we see it passing St. Paul's cathedral while operating for Ensignbus on the Round London Sightseeing Tour and looking extremely smart with appropriate advertisements.

6 August 1983

ABOVE: DMS 620 named Mr Pickwick and numbered CB1 with its new owner Culturebus of Feltham seen in Fleet Street. This service introduced the concept of hop on / hop off to London Sightseeing.

6 August 1983

RIGHT: The rear of DMS 620 with Culturebus as it pauses at the Ludgate Circus traffic lights. This bus would see future service with Ensignbus after the Culturebus operation was purchased and then pass to a Steel Band for their personal transport.

6 August 1983

BELOW: DMS 1476 named General Sirus Choke and carrying fleet number CB3 turns into The Strand at Aldwych. This bus would later see service with Southend Transport.

6 August 1983

TOP: Culturebus CB4 is DMS 589 Major Hannibal Chollop, here it approaches the Law Courts with remarkably little traffic to impede its journey.

6 August 1983

ABOVE: Culturebus CB2 (DMS 1444) Nicholas Nickleby turns into Southampton Row. This bus would later see service with New Enterprise of Tonbridge.

6 August 1983

RIGHT: Probably the smartest bus in the Ensignbus fleet was this DMS 1682, seen here at Victoria in '1933' livery being used on the Round London Sightseeing Tour, note the gold underlined London Transport fleetname, new fleet number and 'Daimler' badge on the front panel.

6 August 1983

LEFT: Following the write-off of DMS 563 (page 40), Swaffham Coachways purchased two DMs as replacements in 1983. Both ran for many years in as acquired LT livery. Here DM 1081 rests in Kings Lynn bus station, the only part of the bus in fleet livery is the yellow engine side cover.

20 August 1983

CENTRE LEFT: Youngs Coaches of Rampton operated a fleet of six DMSs in 1983. In common with other small operators they found Sunday seaside trips lucrative business. Accordingly a summer Sunday would see many Youngs DMSs make the trip to Hunstanton. DMS 2027 in an attractive and unusual livery awaits the return of day trippers in Hunstanton bus station.

21 August 1983

LOWER LEFT: Carrying a full load of Sunday seaside day trippers DMS 2027 of Youngs Coaches leaves Hunstanton bus station.

21 August 1983

LEFT: DMS 1690 was one of three to pass Duncans Coaches of Sawtry, seen here with its back to the sun it stands outside their yard in Huntingdon.

25 August 1983

LEFT: The sunny side of DMS 1690 outside the Huntingdon yard of its new owner Duncans Coaches of Sawtry.

25 August 1983

BELOW: A pair of DMSs belonging to Duncans Coaches at their Huntingdon yard. DMS 1698 stands next to DMS 1690.

25 August 1983

LEFT: The third DMS with Duncans Coaches of Sawtry was to be found at their home address in Sawtry. Here DMS 1678 is moved outside for this photograph to be taken. After its service life with Duncans this bus would later become an exhibition unit for the Fenland Resource Unit based in Wisbech.

25 August 1983

CENTRE: Norfolk Bluebird had a small yard in Ber Street Norwich in the shadow of the castle. They purchased three DMSs in December 1982. DM 1726 stands in their yard. This bus would see later service with operators in Devon and Cornwall.

26 August 1983

LOWER RIGHT: Obscured by advertising boards DM 1712 now with Norfolk Bluebird stands adjacent to Norwich castle in an attempt to attract customers for their daily excursions.

26 August 1983

LEFT: Two of Norfolk Bluebird's DMs 1712 & 1726 parked up for the night in their yard at Ber Street Norwich.

26 August 1983

CENTRE LEFT: On page55, we saw Swaffham Coachways DM 1081, here is their second vehicle DM 1031 in the same spot in Kings Lynn bus station, this bus ran for 4 years in LT livery before being painted yellow and blue.

27 August 1983

LOWER LEFT: Youngs Coaches of Rampton had five DMSs between 2025 and 2033. The first DMS 2025 is seen here in the coach park at Hunstanton during a summer Sunday seaside excursion. The removal of the front destination box was fairly rare at this time.

28 August 1983

LEFT: The scene in Youngs yard at Rampton. Completely burnt out DMS 1501 stands next to DMS 1681 which had been acquired only to provide spares to newer DMSs in the Youngs fleet.
2 September 1983

BELOW: Showbus rally Woburn Abbey, 1983 and typical rain clouds are in evidence, DMS 2051 arrives at the showground now in the ownership of Astill & Jordan Ltd, this bus was the first of five DMSs to be acquired.
4 September 1983

BOTTOM: An acquisition that year by Red Rover Omnibus Company was DMS 2228 bringing the fleet total to five. Here the DMS is being used as rally control at the 1983 Showbus rally at Woburn Abbey with the appropriate destination blind.
4 September 1983

ABOVE: Another Red Rover Omnibus Company DMS at Showbus 1983 was DMS 1919 which was being operated on connecting bus services to the rally site.

4 September 1983

LEFT: To mark fifty years of Autocar at Tunbridge Wells Maidstone & District painted their DMS 2087 in this commemorative livery. It is seen here at the Showbus rally at Woburn Abbey.

4 September 1983

LEFT: A visit to Hornsby Travel at Ashby near Scunthorpe found their then fleet of three DMSs all under cover, here DM 1181 stands in the workshop doorway.

1 October 1983

LEFT: Hornsby were prepared to move one bus outside for me and DMS 1972 was selected as the candidate seen here at their Ashby base, the lack of destination blinds spoils the otherwise smart appearance.

1 October 1983

RIGHT: Moving on from Scunthorpe to Grimsby we find DMS 2077 now Grimsby-Cleethorpes No.1 recently licenced for service taking on passengers in Bethlehem Street Grimsby.

1 October 1983

RIGHT: To Commemorate 100 years of public transport in Grimsby the Grimsby-Cleethorpes Joint Transport Committee painted four DMSs in special liveries. Here DMS 768 wears the green and white colours of Great Grimsby Street Tramways.

1 October 1983

LEFT: Grimsby-Cleethorpes No.8, DM 1176 speeds past Grimsby bus garage. This bus was later shipped to Galway where it continues to provide service in open top form on the sightseeing tour in Galway.

1 October 1983

LEFT: DM 1776 Grimsby-Cleethorpes No. 9 seen here in Grimsby, Riby Square. Most Grimsby DMS saw further service after Grimsby had finished with them and this bus was no exception passing to United Provincial (Pennine Blue) in 1992.

1 October 1983

BELOW: Another Grimsby-Cleethorpes bus that still exists is DM 1141 currently in Dublin as a film support vehicle, in earlier years it stands in Riby Square, Grimsby as their No. 12.

1 October 1983

LEFT: Another view in Riby Square and this time the bus is DM 1089, Grimsby-Cleethorpes No.15, sadly this bus was to be cut up in early 1990.

1 October 1983

LEFT: DM 1070 was to become a familiar sight again in north London when it was rescued from Trevor Wigley's scrap yard by Bryan's of Enfield in 1989. In earlier times it is seen in Riby Square Grimsby.

1 October 1983

LEFT: DM 1151 was one of four DMSs to later pass to United Provincial, here it stands in Grimsby Riby Square as grimsby-Cleethorpes No. 7.

1 October 1983

ABOVE: DMS 2113 was the newest DMS purchased and was to enjoy eight years service in Grimsby before disappearing to a dealer and never seen again in 1991. Here at the familiar terminus, Riby Square it looks very smart having been licensed in June 1983.

1 October 1983

LEFT: DMS 2082 on a grey day in Grimsby as their No. 3 approaches Riby Square. This bus was to finish its days on arduous sightseeing work in New York.

1 October 1983

BELOW: Another of the DMSs painted in special liveries was DMS 778 Grimsby-Cleethorpes No. 18 representing Cleethorpes Corporation, the blue and grey colours make an unusual sight in Freeman Street Grimsby.

1 October 1983

ABOVE: A bright sunny autumn day sees DMSs 646 and 653 stand at Dover Eastern docks awaiting passengers while working for Townsend Thoresen car ferry company.
10 November 1983

RIGHT: Side view of DMS 653 showing the uprising rear stripes at Dover eastern Docks with Townsend Thoresen.
10 November 1983

RIGHT: Hemmed in by the boundary fence and other vehicles at LT's Camberwell garage DMS 1907 was one of two DMSs used by the GLC to publicise welfare rights and both vehicles still exist. This bus is currently serving as a mobile teenage advice centre in Bristol.
26 February 1984

LEFT: In 1984 Ebdons coaches of Sidcup decided to enter the lucrative field of London Sightseeing tours and would eventually purchase 16 DMSs. One of the first three vehicles which were all licensed in March 1984 was DM 1157 seen here being cleaned in the garage yard, it would soon lose its roof and only two years later be sent to Chicago for further sightseeing work.

24 March 1984

LEFT: On Page 60, we saw DMS 2087 at the 1983 Showbus rally in this livery commemorating 50 years of Autocar in Tunbridge Wells, here it is seen in service in Tunbridge Wells High Street.

26 March 1984

BELOW: Maidstone & District NBC livery is applied to DMS 1955 now Maidstone & District 5037 seen in Tunbridge Wells High Street with a Bristol VRT behind.

26 March 1984

LEFT: For over 16 years the Isle of Sheppey played host to DMS 191 at the island playbus which was kept at the main bus station where it is seen. The bus is still on the island, but is now static in a school playground.

29 March 1984

RIGHT: On page48 DMS 1424 was seen on London Sightseeing work with Obsolete fleet in LT red livery. Here freshly painted into white/pink/orange of Emmaheath Ltd but devoid of fleetnames we see it again in Lower Regent Street.

23 April 1984

LEFT: During the annual HCVC London to Brighton run on the first Sunday in May many vehicles travel to Brighton to enjoy a day by the seaside, some vehicles park up for the day in the garage of Brighton Corporation, hence the presence of RM1737. In 1984 Brighton Corporation put some of their own vehicles on show on the garage forecourt. Here their two DMSs are on display. DMS 132 is notable as the being the prototype Leyland engined DMS and is now preserved. DMS 558 went to Scotland for further service in 1986 DMS 558 went to Scotland for further service in 1986

6 May 1984

RIGHT: DM 1710 being prepared for London Sightseeing service in the yard of Ebdons coaches at Sidcup.
7 May 1984

LEFT: The second DMS in the fleet of Davie's of Rye was DM 1725 seen here in their yard.
7 May 1984

RIGHT: Avro & Elm Park coaches of Orsett operated three DMSs, here MCW bodied DM 1705 is seen at Melford Hall while operating a private hire.
27 May 1984

LEFT: Accompanying DM 1705 on the private hire to Melford Hall is PRV bodied DMS 885, all three Avro & Elm Park coaches would pass to Nelson of Wickford in 1987.
27 May 1984

LEFT: On Page27, we saw the original DMS with Wiffens of Finchingfield, here their second example DMS 2094 stand on the village green outside their garage.
28 May 1984

LEFT: Seen at its new home Chartercoach (Harwich), Great Oakley DMS 392 is painted in an all over advert livery for Butlins, Atlas Park.
30 May 1984

LEFT: The other DMS owned by Chartercoach (Harwich) is seen here at the rear of Colchester bus station looking somewhat anonymous it is DM 1719 and is on charter to DFDS Seaways.
31 May 1984

CENTRE LEFT: Osborne of Tollesbury purchased two DMSs in 1983 and a third in 1987. Inside their dark garage we find DM 1228 looking extremely smart.
31 May 1984

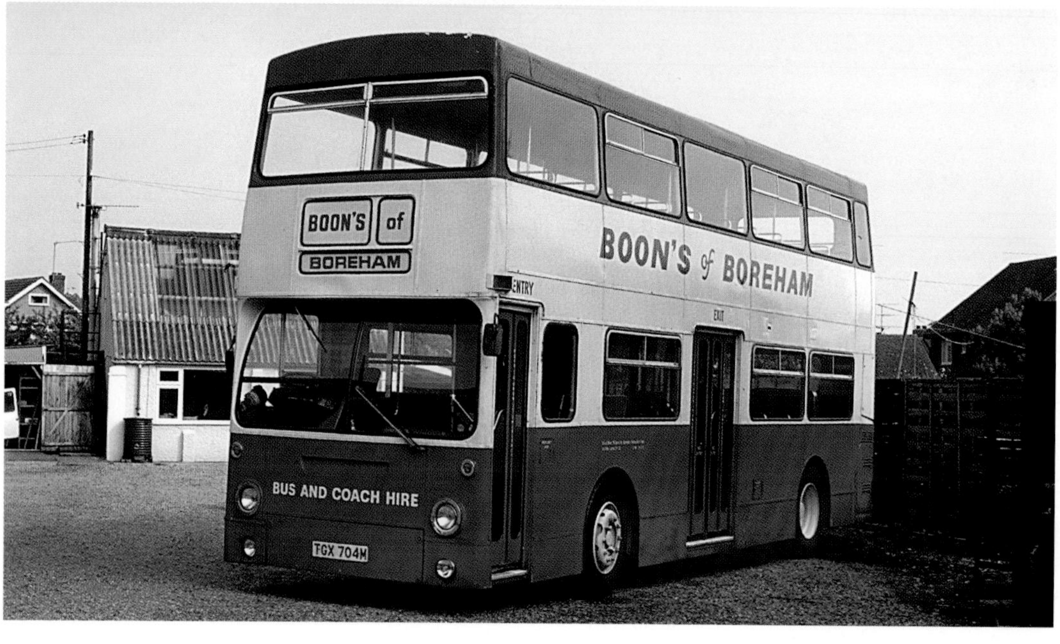

LOWER LEFT: DMS 704 had an interesting conversion to its front door reputably being a trial conversion for DMSs destined for Hong Kong, The additional window at the front can be clearly seen in this view taken in Boons yard at Boreham.
31 May 1984

LEFT: Daly Market Services of Aveley used DMS 1624 for various activities connected to the local market. Here the bus is seen at Epsom Downs on Derby day.

6 June 1984

BELOW: Also at Epsom Downs on Derby day is DMS 1538 being used by Ensignbus on London Sightseeing duties. This bus would later see further service in Oxford and Bath.

6 June 1984

RIGHT: Farleigh Coaches purchased DMS 410 in December 1983 and it was still with them in 2001. Seen here on Epsom Downs on Derby day in its initial livery.

6 June 1984

LEFT: DMS 1256 was seen in London on page6. Seen here in the Richmond yard of Brackell it would pass back to Hewitts Farm, Orpington the following month.
9 June 1984

RIGHT: DMS 1662 stands in the yard of Gastonia Coaches at Cranleigh in this unusual, but striking livery.
9 June 1984

LEFT: Adjacent to Gastonia's yard was a parking area used by hospitality company Bus Fare. DMS 178 is wearing the livery of Shell Oil for a promotion, upper deck curtains can be seen.
9 June 1984

LEFT: on page 68 we saw DM 1710 being prepared for service in Ebdons Sidcup yard. Here the final result is seen at Victoria.

23 June 1984

CENTRE LEFT: Another Ebdons vehicle DM 1113 seen touting for custom on the Victoria stand, like many of its compatriots at Ebdons this bus would later be exported to Chicago.

23 June 1984

RIGHT: From 1984 London sightseeing tour buses started to receive all over advertising liveries. Emmaheath DMS 816 wears Beefeater Gin colours at the Piccadilly stand.

30 June 1984

ABOVE: Behind DMS 816 we find Emmaheath DMS 648 now sporting London Pride fleetnames. Four years later this bus would become a film support vehicle and enjoy a long life not being withdrawn until 1999.
30 June 1984

LEFT: A 1984 delivery to London Cityrama was DMS 1939 seen here in open top form at Piccadilly.
30 June 1984

BELOW: DMS 1667 seen in the yard of Horsham coaches at Warnham station in their attractive livery.
1 July 1984

ABOVE: DMS 855 was being used by the Royal Shakespeare Company when seen here parked in Holborn.
6 July 1984

LEFT: Offside view of DMS 855 seen in Holborn while promoting the Royal Shakespeare Company.
6 July 1984

BELOW: DMS 586 with Ebdons Tours speeds past St. Pauls Cathedral with a good load.
6 July 1984

LEFT: In the same spot by St. Pauls Cathedral we see Ebdons DM 1218.

6 July 1984

BELOW: Ebdons retained the roof on DM 1138, but removed the upper deck windows and named the vehicle a photobus. It passes the coach park at St. Pauls Cathedral.

6 July 1984

BOTTOM: Another 1984 delivery to London Cityrama was DMS 2029 which retained its roof, it would later be converted to part open top at the rear. It is seen passing St. Pauls Cathedral.

6 July 1984

RIGHT: The Southampton garage of Hamshire Bus sees two DMS in NBC livery. DMS 2039 stands behind DMS 2245 now numbered 1926 & 1917, interestingly these are the oldest and newest DMSs in their fleet.

8 July 1984

BELOW: Three more Hampshire Bus DMS in the Southampton yard, DMSs 2040, 2197 & 2194, these and other vehicles from this fleet would later become part of the Stagecoach fleet and move to Carlisle.

8 July 1984

BOTTOM: The modern architecture of Southampton provides the backdrop as Hampshire bus 1923, DMS 2169 leaves the Bus station.

8 July 1984

LEFT: Coach Services of Thetford woul
operate three DMSs in service. their sec
ond bus was DM 1798 seen here i
Thetford Bus station.
24 July 1984

LEFT: DMS 556 passed through vari
ous dealers and operators and is no
thought to have seen much if any serv
ice use. Here parked out of use in th
yard of Coach Services at Thetfor
being cannibalised, it would be scrappe
later in the year.
24 July 1984

BELOW: DM 924 won an award for it
colour scheme, here it pauses for th
camera as it leave the yard of Coac
Services in Thetford.
24 July 1984

RIGHT: Norfolk Bluebird DM 1726 takes on passengers outside Norwich castle.
27 July 1984

CENTRE RIGHT: DM 1712 seen in Norwich with an Eastern Counties Bristol VRT behind, after use by Norfolk Bluebird this bus would pass in 1985 to Normenda Travel in Hampshire seeing only sporadic use before being sold to Ensignbus in 2001.
27 July 1984

BELOW: A summer Sunday in Hunstanton sees Youngs of Rampton DMSs 2033 and 2025 on a day trip in the coach park.
29 July 1984

LEFT: The original livery carried by DMS 2192 acquired earlier in the year by Morleys of Whittlesey when seen at Whittlesey market place, the following year a second DMS would be purchased and both vehicles would still be owned in 2001.

1 August 1984

ABOVE: DM 1747 is seen in Leicester high street now 2747 in the fleet of Midland Fox carrying an all over advertisement for Brolac paint.

11 August 1984

LEFT: Midland Fox 2781, DM 1781 seen in Leicester high street with an all over advertisement for 'Y' fronts. This pass would later operate with associated company Wreake valley before being scrapped by Norths in early 1992.

11 August 1984

RIGHT: Licensed only the previous month DMS 1927 is seen in full Midland Fox livery in Leicester Haymarket.
11 August 1984

BELOW: Still in original Midland Red East plain red livery, but with Midland Fox fleetnames added DM 1744 stands in Abbey Street Leicester.
11 August 1984

RIGHT: One of the DMSs acquired from London Country where it had been a driver trainer is DMS 631 seen in Abbey Street Leicester back in public service with Midland Fox.
11 August 1984

LEFT: Contrasting liveries by two Midland Fox DMSs in Abbey Street Leicester. DMS 1994 in full fleet livery is being followed by DMS 1912.

11 August 1984

BELOW: DMS 1912 in Abbey Road Leicester while Midland Fox No. 2893 with an all over advertisement for National Travelworld.

11 August 1984

LEFT: A very smart looking DM 1730 in the Midland Fox fleet although it has yet to receive the yellow/red livery, it collects passengers in Abbey Street Leicester.

11 August 1984

ABOVE: DM 1755 with Midland Fox seen in Abbey Street Leicester.

11 August 1984

LEFT: Licensed the previous month DMS 1961 is seen in full Midland Fox livery in Abbey Street Leicester.

11 August 1984

BELOW: This bus, the former DMS 1782, would later join the fleet of New York Apple Tours, in earlier times, DM 1782 is seen in Leicester Abbey Street in the fleet of Midland Fox.

11 August 1984

LEFT: Another vehicle to see further service with Wreake Valley is this bus DM 1772 seen here in Abbey Street Leicester carrying an all over advertisement for National Holidays.

11 August 1984

LEFT: Astill & Jordan acquired DMS 2043 from Stevensons in 1983. It stands behind a similar vehicle with Midland Fox in Charles Street Leicester, note the removal of the panels above the engine compartment which allows the lower rear window to be cleaned more easily.

11 August 1984

BELOW: The first DMS of many in the Mayne's of Manchester fleet is DMS 2163 acquired from Stevensons in their dealer capacity seen leaving their garage.

18 August 1984

ABOVE LEFT: Also to see further service with Stevensons, DMS 710 is shown here withdrawn inside Greater Manchester Swinton garage.
18 August 1984

ABOVE: The DMSs with Lancashire United Transport only saw four or five years use although some saw further use with other operators. Recently withdrawn DMS 635 inside Atherton garage would re-enter service with Stevensons.
18 August 1984

LEFT: Still in service with Greater Manchester DMS 1489 is seen inside Swinton garage still carrying the livery of Lancashire United the early type of centre door removal can also be seen.
18 August 1984

LEFT: DMS 1452 had only two months more service with Greater Manchester to go, seen here inside Swinton garage.
18 August 1984

ABOVE: On page 72 we saw this bus in the Richmond yard of Brackell. Here at its new home of Hewitts farm in Orpington is DMS 1256. This was used to bring members of the public to the farm where they could pick their own fruit.

18 August 1984

RIGHT: The Showbus rally at Woburn Abbey sees Thamesdown 126, DMS 2215 in their original livery having been licensed only the previous day.

2 September 1984

BELOW: DMS 2209 was purchased by Platignum of Stevenage for staff transport seen here parked outside the factory. This bus would later pass to Red Rover for further service.

2 September 1984

ABOVE: On page 31 we saw DMS 457 in Stevensons fleet livery, three years later it was carrying this all over advertisement livery for Stevensons Travel as it manoeuvres in Uttoxeter bus station.

8 September 1984

LEFT: Stevensons No. 38 DMS 298 collects passengers in Uttoxeter bus station.

8 September 1984

BELOW: DMS 40 was purchased by Stevensons merely to provide spares for the rest of the fleet. It stands in the Spath yard next to the prototype B45 Olympian.

8 September 1984

TOP: Acquired by Stevensons earlier in the year was DMS 2047, seen on the left in this view at the Spath yard. It is shown being prepared for an all over advertisement for Toons Carpet warehouse. DMS 314, now Stevensons No. 42 was parked to the right.

8 September 1984

ABOVE: DM 1716 & 1764 represent the Stevensons fleet in the yard at Spath.

8 September 1984

LEFT: DMS 1251 had been in service with Stevensons for just over two years when this photograph was taken in Uttoxeter bus station, the addition of 'bumpers' on the front lower corner panels is interesting.

8 September 1984

ABOVE: Stevensons no. 44 is DMS 1315 seen here in Uttoxeter bus station carrying an all over advertisement for the Burton Trader newspaper.
8 September 1984

RIGHT: DMS 2133 would later pass to Midland Fox for further service. Here in Uttoxeter bus station as Stevensons No. 26 it carries an all over advertisement for a Volvo dealer in Burton on Trent.
8 September 1984

RIGHT: A collection of vehicles in Stevensons Burton on Trent yard, at the front is DMS 196 and behind is DMS 584 recently acquired from GMPTE. It would be almost a year before the latter vehicle entered service with Stevensons.
8 September 1984

TOP: DMS 1460 bought from GMPTE (Lancashire United) seen in the Burton on Trent yard of Stevensons next to DMS 1711. DMS 1460 would pass to Astill & Jordan the following year before returning again to Stevensons for further service with them from 1986. **8 September 1984**

ABOVE: DMS 2044 was acquired from Ensignbus in January 1983, but would not enter service with Stevensons until October 1985. It stands in their Burton on Trent yard next to DMS 584 acquired from GMPTE (Lancashire United) which would return to service with Stevensons in November 1985. **8 September 1984**

BELOW LEFT: DMS 307 was acquired by Stevensons for spares only it is seen in the Burton on Trent yard behind DMS 196. **8 September 1984**

BELOW RIGHT: Retaining London Transport livery DMS 2042 is parked in the Burton on Trent yard of Stevensons. **8 September 1984**

ABOVE LEFT: Another view of DMS 1460 (see previous page.)
8 September 1984

ABOVE RIGHT: Four months after this photograph was taken in Stevensons Burton on Trent yard, DMS 2131 would pass to Maynes of Manchester for their use. DMS 307 was not so fortunate passing to the scrapyard the following year.
8 September 1984

LEFT: Wetmore Park bus station in Burton on Trent sees DMS 1974 now Stevensons No. 34 with an advert for their X38 express service to Birmingham.
8 September 1984

BELOW: DMS 465 was one of the vehicles delivered with two piece front entrance doors. Seen here in Derby city centre as their No. 257.
8 September 1984

RIGHT: Looking almost new DM 1004 is now London Sightseeing Tours No. 6, it stands alongside LT's Victoria garage in what was known as Wilton Road coach station. It was working on the Round London Sightseeing Tour.
15 September 1984

RIGHT: On the same day in Wilton Road coach station we find DMS 2222 in the ownership of Holman Bros, a couple of years later this bus would move north for further service with Mercer's of Preston.
15 September 1984

BELOW: Not pictured previously is Ebdons of Sidcup DMS 853 working on their Round London Sightseeing Service awaiting custom at Victoria.
15 September 1984

ABOVE: London Sightseeing Tour No.4 is DMS 1944 standing in Park Lane at a stop still used today for London sightseeing by the Big Bus Company.

15 September 1984

LEFT: In the same spot as DMS 816 (see page 74) we now find DMS 840 with Emmaheath also in an all over advertisement for Beefeater Gin. This bus would meet its end by providing spares in New York.

15 September 1984

LEFT: Emmaheath trading as London Pride Sightseeing Tours were using DMS 1469 in this view at Piccadilly, this bus would have a new life as an exhibition vehicle and would be extensively rebuilt by Ensignbus. It still exists in 2001.

15 September 1984

RIGHT: On 24 March 1984 DM1157 was pictured in Ebdons Sidcup yard with its roof intact. Six months later it is now in open top form when seen at Victoria, like many other Ebdons DMSs this bus would later be exported for further service in Chicago.
15 September 1984

BELOW: DMS 1610 now JR12 with Western SMT seen in Gauze Street Paisley complete with Scottish style front blind box. This vehicle would later return to London for service with Bexleybus.
6 October 1984

BOTTOM: Graham's bus services of Paisley would eventually operate over 20 DMSs. A day trip from Kent produced their DMS 1451 seen in their garage yard with the early type of centre door removal.
6 October 1984

TOP: DMS 668 seen in the yard of Graham's bus services at Paisley.
6 October 1984

ABOVE: A smart looking DMS 2057 having been licensed only a few days before by Graham's bus services of Paisley speeds along Gauze Street Paisley.
6 October 1984

LEFT: Another vehicle to return to London for the Bexleybus operation is DMS 1656 seen here in Paisley as Western Scottish No. JR 14.
6 October 1984

RIGHT: Graham's bus services of Paisley would operate DMS 665 for two more years before passing it Clyde Coast in Ardrossen. It is seen here in Paisley Gauze Street.

6 October 1984

BELOW: JR 991 in the western Scottish fleet was DMS 1492 seen here in Gauze Street Paisley before its return to London three years later.

6 October 1984

RIGHT: Graham's bus services of Paisley DMS 2137 in Gauze Street Paisley, this bus would have a varied future operating for Amberley Coaches in Leeds and Tame Valley in Birmingham.

6 October 1984

LEFT : DMS 1596 still exists as an exhibition bus in Dundee, here it is seen as Graham's bus services No. D29 in Gauze Street.

6 October 1984

LEFT: DMS 1505 now Western Scottish JR 985 seen in Gauze Street Paisley, this bus would pass to Clydeside Scottish, but would then be scrapped in early 1986.

6 October 1984

BELOW: Another view of DMS 1656 seen here in Paisley as Western Scottish No. JR 14. 6 October 1984 before its eventual return to London for the Bexleybus operation.

6 October 1984

INDEX – Buses are indexed by fleet number, followed by the date on which that bus was photographed, each caption showing the date to make for easy reference with all photos in date order.

DMS/DM class no.	Date of photograph(s)
23	03.02.80
40	08.09.84
132	06.05.84
178	09.06.83
191	29.03.84
196	07.09.80
	29.08.81
	08.09.84
240	03.02.80
241	29.08.81 x2
298	29.08.81 x 2
	08.09.84
307	08.09.84
314	29.08.81
	08.09.84
362	29.08.81
392	30.05.84
399	25.08.80
405	25.08.80
408	06.08.83
410	06.06.84
415	07.09.80
416	01.08.81 x 2
419	24.04.80
422	01.08.81
437	24.04.80 x 2
438	13.04.80 x 3
441	22.07.80
457	29.08.81 x 2
	08.09.84
465	22.07.80
	29.08.81
	08.09.84
481	03.02.80
553	25.09.82
555	01.08.81 x 2
556	24.07.84
558	06.05.84
561	01.08.81 x 2
563	29.07.82
568	22.07.80
571	05.06.83
584	08.09.84 x 2
586	06.07.84
	25.09.82
589	06.08.83
597	18.05.80 x 2
606	25.08.80
620	06.08.83 x 2
624	07.09.80
626	25.08.80
	26.10.80
631	11.08.84
635	18.08.84
641	03.07.81
646	10.11.83
648	30.06.84
653	25.08.80
	07.09.80 x 2
	10.11.83 x 2
663	25.08.80 x 2
665	06.10.84
668	06.10.84
677	19.08.81
695	26.10.80
701	01.06.81
704	31.05.84
706	25.09.82
710	18.08.84
729	06.06.82
734	22.07.80
738	25.09.82
744	25.09.82
759	25.09.82
768	01.10.83
778	01.10.83
792	21.11.81
816	30.06.84
840	15.09.84

DMS/DM class no.	Date of photograph(s)
853	15.09.84
855	06.07.84 x 2
885	27.05.84
924	24.07.84
927	17.07.82
961	17.07.82
1004	15.09.84
1018	20.08.83
1031	27.08.83
1070	01.10.83
1081	20.08.83
1089	01.10.83
1107	17.07.82
1113	23.06.84
1138	06.07.84
1141	01.10.83
1151	01.10.83
1157	24.03.84
	15.09.84
1175	05.06.83
1176	01.10.83
1181	01.10.83
1211	25.09.82 x 2
1215	05.06.83
1218	06.07.84
1228	31.05.84
1250	13.05.79
1251	13.05.79
1252	01.08.81 x 2
1255	13.05.79 x 2
	23.05.80
1256	13.05.79
	03.06.79
	22.07.79
	09.06.84
	18.08.84
1257	22.07.79
1258	13.05.79
1259	13.05.79 x 2
1260	13.05.79 x 2
	12.08.79
1261	13.05.79 x 2
	23.05.80
1262	13.05.79
1263	13.05.79
	01.08.81
1264	21.05.79
1265	13.05.79
	22.08.79
	12.09.81
1266	19.05.79
	21.05.79
1267	21.05.79
	03.06.79
	22.08.79 x 2
1268	21.05.79
1270	23.05.80
1271	23.05.80
1272	23.05.80
1273	23.05.80
1274	12.09.81
1275	22.08.79
	12.09.81
1276	22.07.79 x 3
	23.05.80
1278	23.05.80
1279	23.05.80
1283	29.08.81
1284	29.08.81
1285	06.08.80
1291	12.08.79
1294	12.08.79
1297	12.08.79
1298	01.08.81
1303	29.08.81
1304	04.06.80
	07.09.80
	09.06.84
1307	07.09.80

DMS/DM class no.	Date of photograph(s)
1310	23.05.80
1315	08.09.84
1317	23.05.80
1324	03.02.80
1329	23.05.80
1338	23.05.80
1343	12.09.81
1349	23.05.80
1352	12.09.81
1354	23.05.80
1358	23.05.80
1364	25.08.80
1371	07.09.80
	12.09.81
1402	07.09.80
1412	25.09.82
1414	13.04.80 x 2
1415	22.07.80
1417	25.09.82
1423	01.08.81
1424	07.04.83
	23.04.84
1428	25.09.82
1432	25.09.82
1434	25.09.82
1443	25.09.82
1444	06.08.83
1448	01.08.81 x 2
1451	06.10.84
1452	18.08.84
1460	08.09.84 x 2
1469	15.09.84
1475	01.08.81
1476	06.08.83
1489	18.08.84
1492	06.10.84
1501	30.07.82
	02.09.83
1505	06.10.84
1526	26.10.80
1538	06.06.84
1552	17.10.81
1581	28.06.81
1584	17.10.81
1586	17.10.81
1596	06.10.84
1601	30.05.82
1610	06.10.84
1624	06.06.84
1656	06.10.84 x 2
1657	06.10.84
1662	17.07.82
	09.06.84
1667	17.07.82
	01.07.84
1678	25.08.83
1681	02.09.83
1682	06.08.83
1690	25.08.83 x 3
1692	02.06.82
1693	22.05.83
1698	25.08.83
1705	27.05.84
1708	29.08.81
1710	07.05.84
	23.06.84
1711	29.08.81 x 2
	08.09.84
1712	26.08.83 x 2
	27.07.84
1716	29.08.81
	08.09.84
1719	31.05.84
1720	06.08.83
1725	07.05.84
1726	26.08.83 x 2
	27.07.84
1730	11.08.84
1744	11.08.84

DMS/DM class no.	Date of photograph(s)
1747	11.08.84
1748	28.08.82
1755	11.08.84
1758	17.07.82
1761	28.08.82
1764	08.09.84
1765	31.10.81
1769	28.08.82
1772	11.08.84
1776	01.10.83
1778	28.08.82
1780	17.07.82
1782	11.08.84
1781	11.08.84
1785	03.10.82
1798	24.07.84
1907	26.02.84
1912	11.08.84
1919	04.09.83
1927	11.08.84
1939	30.06.84
1940	18.06.83
1944	15.09.84
1955	18.06.83
	26.03.84
1961	11.08.84
1972	01.10.83
1974	08.09.84
1994	11.08.84
2021	06.10.84
2025	28.08.83
	29.07.84
2027	21.08.8 3 x 2
2029	06.07.84
2033	29.07.84
2039	08.07.84
2040	08.07.84
2042	08.09.84
2043	11.08.84
2044	08.09.84
2047	08.09.84
2051	04.09.83
2057	06.10.84
2061	06.11.82
2066	06.06.82
2070	01.10.83
2077	01.10.83
2082	01.10.83
2087	04.09.83
	26.03.84
2090	18.06.83
2091	06.08.83
2094	28.05.84
2101	22.08.82
2104	06.08.83
2113	01.10.83
2127	07.04.83
2129	06.10.84
2131	08.09.84
2133	08.09.84
2137	06.10.84
2148	06.08.83 x 2
2150	17.07.82
2163	06.06.82
	18.08.84
2169	08.07.84
2192	01.08.84
2194	08.07.84
2197	08.07.84
2209	02.09.84
2215	02.09.84
2222	15.09.84
2228	04.09.83
2233	01.06.83
2245	08.07.84

SYPTE1511 25.09.82

For ease of reference, where more than one date is given, the second and subsequent dates are offset to the right to highlight this.